Little Mitchie

STRANGE PLACES

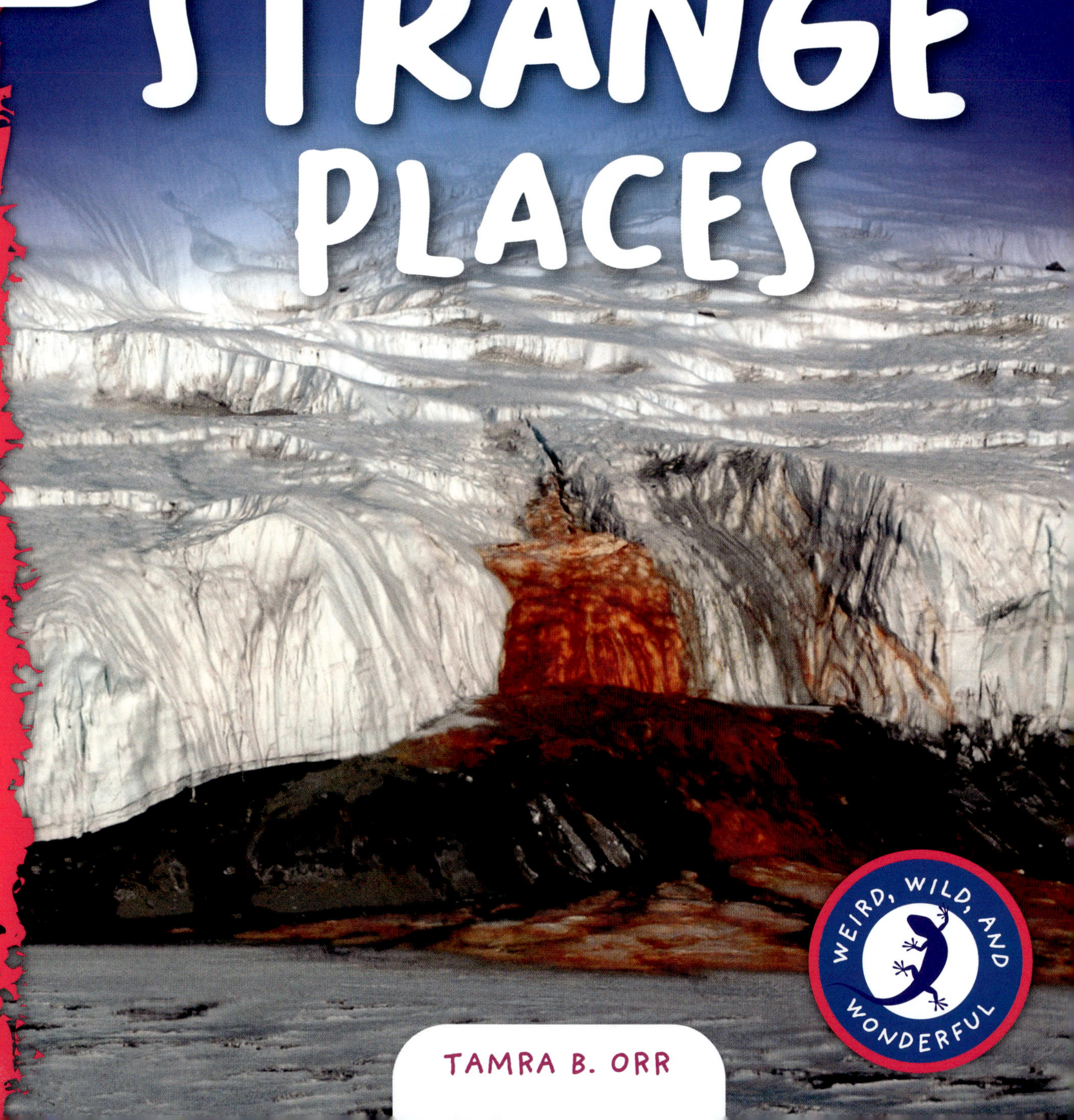

WEIRD, WILD, AND WONDERFUL

TAMRA B. ORR

CREATING YOUNG NONFICTION READERS

Little Mitchie books spark curiosity and support early nonfiction reading for students in Grades 2-3. Designed to build vocabulary, support second language learners, and prepare readers for middle-grade content, each book includes helpful tips for parents and educators to build confidence and deepen understanding of the world.

TIPS FOR READING NONFICTION WITH BEGINNING READERS

Talk about Nonfiction

Begin by explaining that nonfiction books give us information that is true. The book will be organized around a specific topic or idea, and we may learn new facts through reading.

Look at the Parts

Most nonfiction books have helpful features. Our *Little Mitchie* titles include color photographs and graphic aids, a table of contents, a glossary, and an index. Share the purpose of these features with your reader.

Color Photos and Graphic Aids

A lot of information can be found by "reading" photos, charts, maps, and other graphic aids found within nonfiction texts. Help your reader learn more about the different ways information can be displayed.

Table of Contents

Located at the front of the book, this list shows the big ideas within the text and the page numbers where they can be found.

Glossary

Located at the back of the book, the glossary defines key words and phrases that are related to the topic. These words and phrases can be found in the text in colored type.

Index

Located at the back of the book, an index is an alphabetical list of topics and the page numbers where they can be found.

With a little help and guidance about reading nonfiction, you can feel good about introducing a young reader to the world of *Little Mitchie* nonfiction books.

Little Mitchie is an imprint of:

Mitchell Lane
PUBLISHERS

2001 SW 31st Avenue
Hallandale, FL 33009
mitchelllanepub.com

First Edition, 2027.

Author: Tamra B. Orr
Designer: Jen Bowers
Editor: Tricia Hoffman
Library of Congress Cataloging-in-Publication Data
Title: Strange Places / by Tamra Orr

Description: Hallandale, FL :
Mitchell Lane Publishers, [2027]

Identifiers:
ISBN 979-8-89260-894-7 (library bound)
ISBN 979-8-89260-997-5 (eBook)

Library of Congress Control Number: 2026936384

PHOTO CREDITS
cover, p.1, p.7 Public Domain/National Science Foundation/Peter Rejcek; Shutterstock: p.5 ©2020 defmodel1, p.7 ©2018 Shaun Jeffers, p.8–9 ©2018 Pedro Alvera, p.10 ©2022 Paul Brady Photography, p.11 ©2019 matteo_it, p.12 ©2013 Fotos593, p.13 ©2022 Marcin Mierzejewski, p.14 ©2018 Guillermo Caffarini, p.15 © 2009 R Gombarik, p.16–17 ©2017 L_B_Photography, p.19 ©2016 Drone Explorer, p.20 ©2025 Shutterstock AI, p.22 ©2017 Naeblys, ©2017 sido kagawa, ©2024 marketa1982

TABLE OF CONTENTS

Chapter One

STRANGE EARTH

This planet has beautiful places that amaze and inspire. But some places can surprise and even frighten! Visiting from the safety of a book is a great way to explore.

THE WAVE IS A NATURAL ROCK FORMATION IN ARIZONA.

NATURE AND HUMANS

Some of the world's strangest places were made by Mother Nature. Others were created by people.

Chapter Two

IT'S ALL NATURAL

Exploring caves usually means bringing a flashlight. But not in New Zealand! Some caves there have thousands of fly **larvae**. These glowworms shine a blue-green light to attract tasty insects.

BLOOD FALLS

Antarctica is covered in white snow and ice. But in 1911, explorers spotted a waterfall gushing bright red water! Later, scientists discovered the color was because of iron salts contacting oxygen.

Scattered across Namibia's desert are millions of fairy circles, ranging from 12 to 114 feet (3.6 to 34.7 m) in **diameter**. Who made these bare spots? Some people say fairies. Scientists think it was actually **termites**!

SAILING STONES

Each winter, huge rocks mysteriously move across the frozen ground of Death Valley National Park in California. Scientists found that when the ice under these "sailing stones" melted, the winds blew the ice sheets. It carried the rocks with them.

In Australia, Lake Hillier is hard to find but impossible to forget. The lake is eight times saltier than the ocean. That saltiness, along with bacteria and **algae**, make this lake bright pink!

Chapter Three

THANKS TO HUMANS

Some of Earth's strangest places are man-made. Flying over Peru, you can see hundreds of ancient, white-lined **geoglyphs**. About 2,000 years ago, the Nazca people created these giant pictures by moving rocks and dirt to show the lighter earth underneath.

UPSIDE DOWN

People from all over the world come to explore the upside-down house in Poland. Its roof is on the ground and its foundation is in the air! This silly house is also full of upside-down furniture.

Chile's Atacama Desert has miles and miles of sand. But in the middle is a 36-foot (11-m) hand reaching up from the ground! The sculpture was made in 1992.

UNDERWATER WONDERS

Sculptures are common in most museums. But in Grenada's Molinere Bay, many sculptures are set up underwater! They act as **artificial** coral reefs. Octopuses, lobsters, and other marine creatures make them their home.

In Nevada's Black Rock Desert, there is a **geyser** that was made by accident! People were drilling for water when very hot, mineral-filled water burst from the ground. Over the years, the minerals built up, creating colorful cone-shaped mounds.

Chapter Four

UNSOLVED MYSTERIES

One of the world's most famous landmarks is a mystery! England's Stonehenge is a circle of huge stones built 5,000 years ago. How did people move stones weighing up to 48,500 pounds (22 t)? No one knows!

IT'S A MYSTERY

Scientists and explorers study the world's most mysterious places. They want to understand how they were created. Sometimes, decades pass and no one can find an answer!

SO STRANGE!

Each year, experts discover new answers to old mysteries. They do experiments. They interview others. Slowly, they find answers. But until then, people will keep marveling at how some places in the world are so strange!

The Bermuda Triangle in the Atlantic Ocean is a place of mystery. Many airplanes and ships have gone missing there. Some people think storms or giant waves caused the disappearances. But no one knows for sure!

EVEN WILDER!

Socotra Island in Yemen has some strange plants. It is home to ancient dragon's blood trees and bulbous bottle trees!

Cat Island in Japan is an island with more cats than people. There are about 20 cats for every one person!

The Island of the Dolls is a strange place in Mexico. The island is home to more than 1,000 dolls hanging from trees!

GLOSSARY

algae (al-jee) small plants without roots or stems that grow mainly in water

artificial (ahr-tuh-fish-uhl) made by people rather than existing in nature

diameter (dye-am-i-tur) a straight line through the center of a circle

geoglyphs (jee-oh-glifs) large patterns or designs on the surface of land, made by arranging stones or earth

geyser (gye-zur) an underground hot spring that shoots boiling water and steam into the air

larvae (lahr-vee) insects at the stage of development after they hatch from eggs, when they look like worms

termites (tur-mites) insects that feed on wood

FURTHER READING

O'Neill, Bill. *The Ultimate Book of Random Fun Facts.* LAK Publishing, 2024.

Spilsbury, Louise. *Earth's Strangest Places.* Cheriton Children's Books, 2024.

ON THE INTERNET

Wackiest Places Around the World
https://kids.nationalgeographic.com/videos/topic/wackiest-places-around-the-world
Watch videos to explore some of the strangest places in the world with National Geographic Kids.

Top 25 Interesting Geography Facts For Kids
www.parentcircle.com/interesting-fun-geography-facts-for-kids/article
Check out fun facts about everything from volcanoes to islands.

INDEX